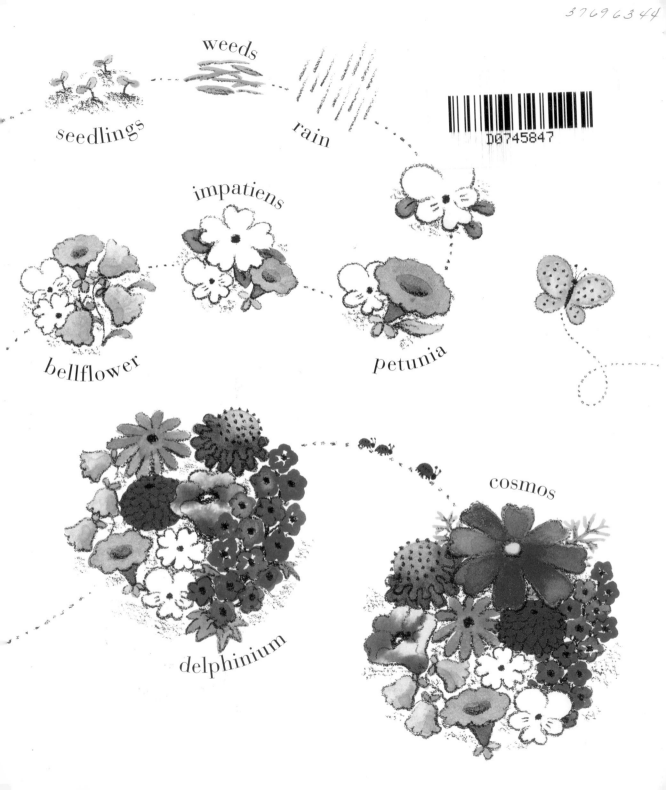

seedlings

weeds

rain

impatiens

bellflower

petunia

delphinium

cosmos

This Is Your Garden

Maggie Smith

Crown Publishers, Inc., New York

This is your garden.
It is yours and yours alone.
It is yours for keeps.

These are the things you will need
        for your garden:
        your own space for planting,
        good tools,
        and seeds.

Some seeds you may get from
        your friends and family.
Some you will find in the backyard.

Others you will find
inside your own pocket.

First, make a nice soft bed in the ground.
Dig the warm soil and take out any big stones.

Scatter the seeds,
or place them in rows.

Then cover them up with a blanket of earth.

Now they'll need water and sun,
    light and time.
You can tell them a story
    or sing them a song of encouragement.

    Soon tiny seedlings
        will poke up their heads
            to see what's going on
                out there.

They will be very delicate at first,
   so you will need to protect them.
Pull up any weeds
   that try to crowd them out.

Shoo out the crows
and bugs that might harm
your seedlings.

As the little plants grow,
   some will be straight
   and some will be wobbly.
Some might be thirstier than others.

But they will all need you.

                 This is your garden.

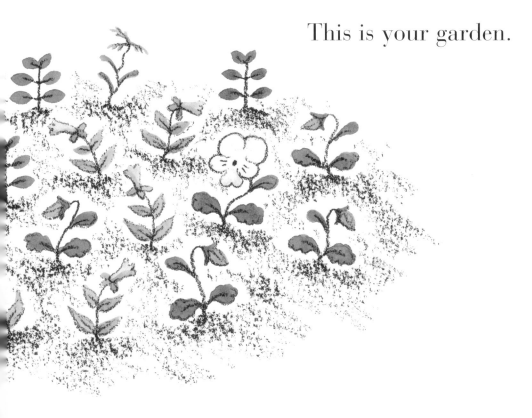

There will be days
    when it's dark and rainy
        and you can't tend to your garden.

You can stay inside with
    your favorite book,

and know that your garden
is getting a good soaking.

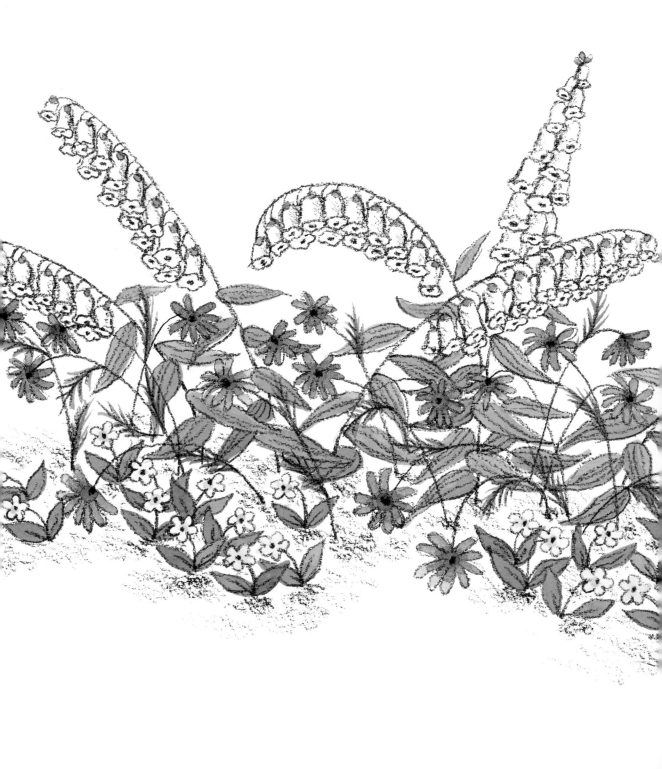

But sometimes, even if it's sunny,
  you may wander through other gardens
  to see what's growing there.

In some gardens a quick peek is enough.

But in others you could stay all day.
They may have flowers
    you want to grow in your garden too.

Your garden will wait for you,
and it will always
be happy to see you
when you return.

As your garden grows fuller,
   you may need to thin some things out.
You can kiss them good-bye
   and say you'll visit on Thursdays.

Now there is room
for the old plants to flourish

and space to add
something
new.

If you think that your garden
is not growing fast enough,
do not worry.

Give it plenty of water,
let the light shine—
and your garden will grow…

...in its own perfect time.

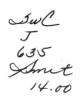
For Jessica

Happy growing!

Library of Congress Cataloging-in-Publication Data
Smith, Maggie, 1965–
This is your garden / Maggie Smith. — 1st ed.
p. cm.
Summary: A little girl, given good tools and seeds, begins to grow a garden that needs
water, sun, weeding, and her encouragement.
ISBN 0-517-70992-9. (trade). — ISBN 0-517-70993-7 (lib. bdg.)
1. Gardening—Juvenile literature. [1. Gardening.] I. Title.
SB457.S68 1998 635—dc21 97-31963
10 9 8 7 6 5 4 3 2 1
First Edition